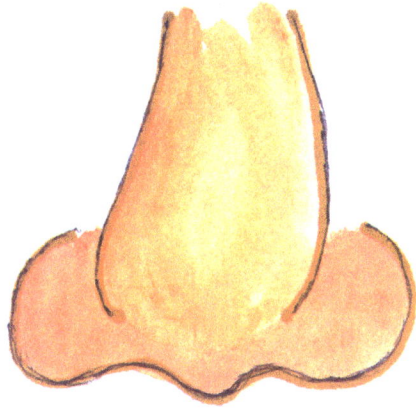

The Nose Book

by

Annette Chaudet

Copyright 2006 Annette Chaudet

ISBN# 978-1-932636-36-9 Softcover

Library of Congress Control Number: 2007933680

Book Design: Antelope Design
Illustrated by the Author

Prairie
Winkle

an imprint of Pronghorn Press
www.pronghornpress.org

Sometimes
nonsense
makes
sense

i've
heard
it's
been
said...

and
it's
oft
been
repeated:

a

rose

is

a

rose

is

a

rose.

So,
if
that's
the case...

it
might
be
concluded

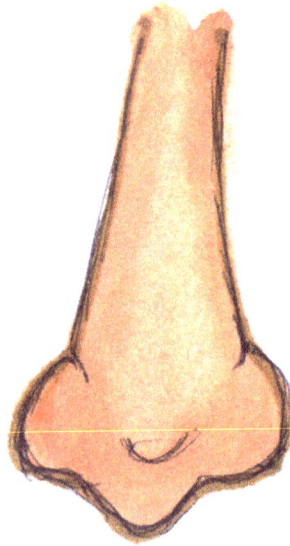

a

nose

is

a

nose

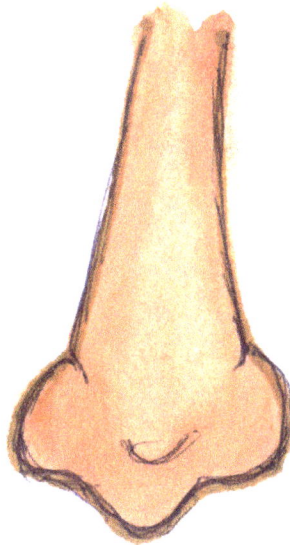

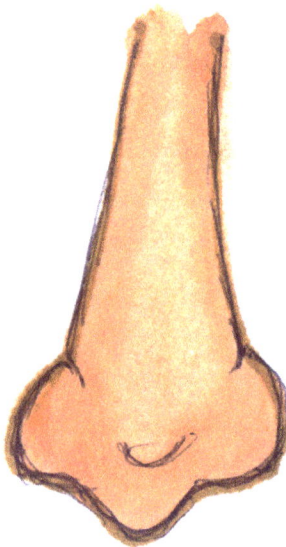

is

a

nose.

But
we all
know
that
noses

come
in

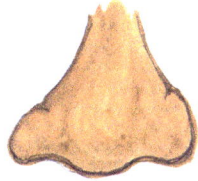
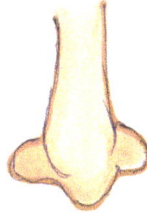
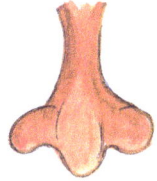

a

dozen

designs,

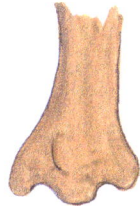

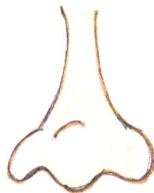
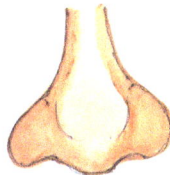

not
to
mention

the

sizes.

So,

if

a

nose

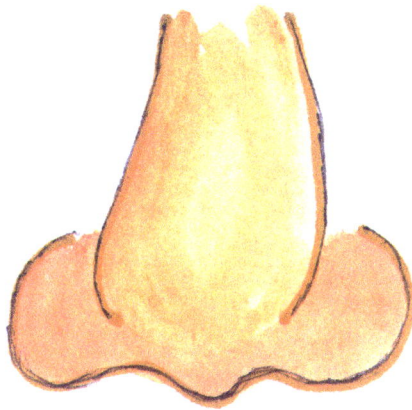

we're
simply
a
nose

it
would
be
one of
Life's
great
surprises!

Yet
all
noses
share

certain afflictions

like
sneezes
and

sniffles
and
wheezes.

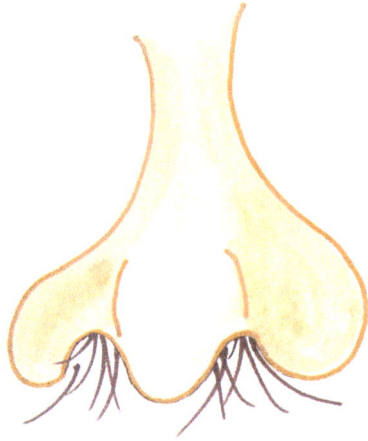

And
some
noses
have
far too many hairs

and
require
a pair
of the
tweezers!

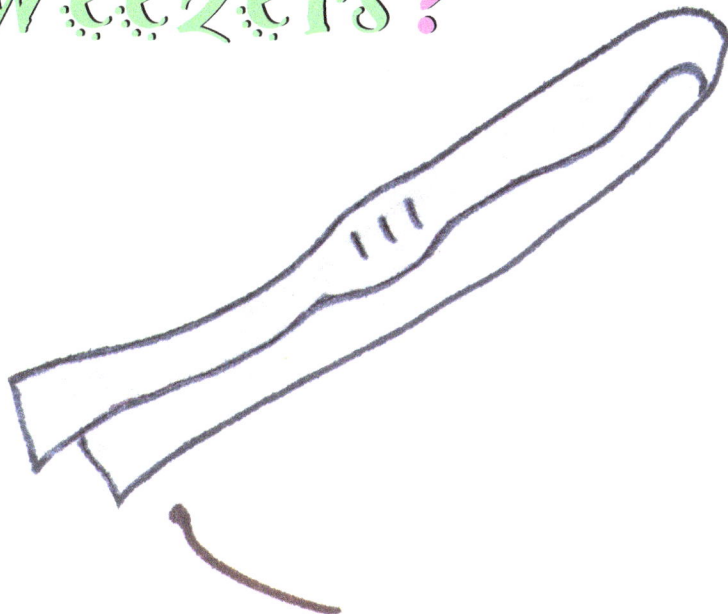

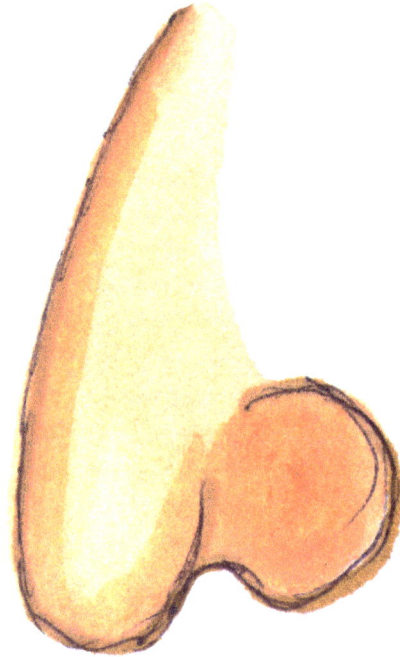

Some
noses
are
big.

Some noses are small.

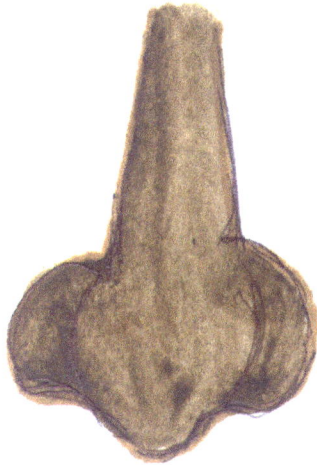

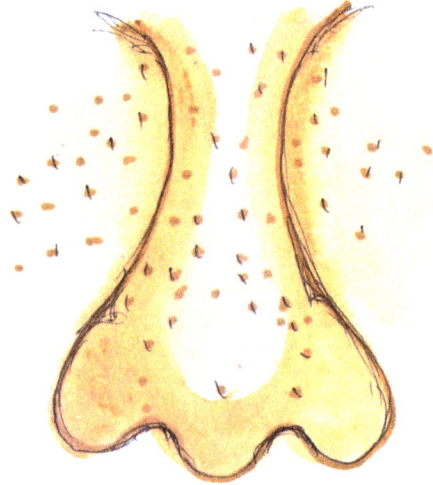

Some
are covered
with
freckely spots.

Some noses are red.

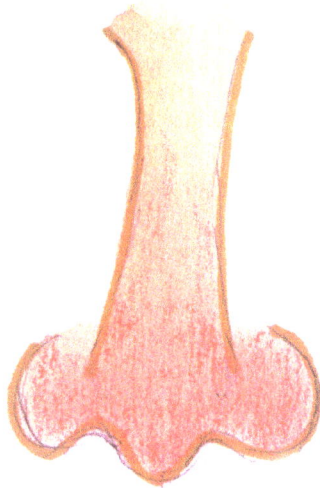

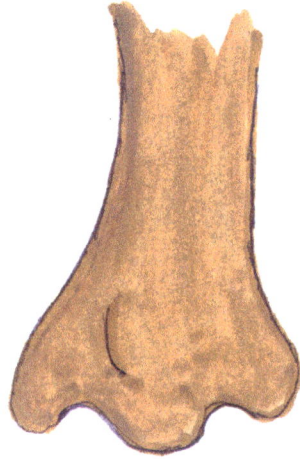

Some noses
are
brown.

Some
noses
have
wrinkles
... lots!

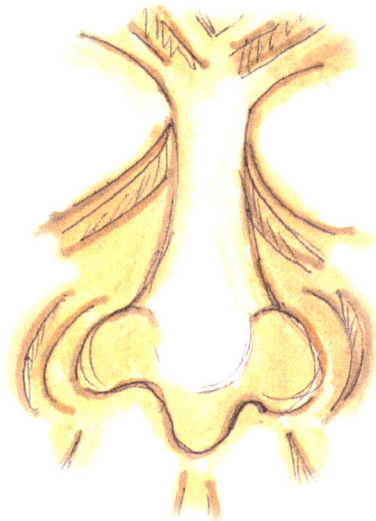

Some
noses
seem
plain

while
others
have
rings.

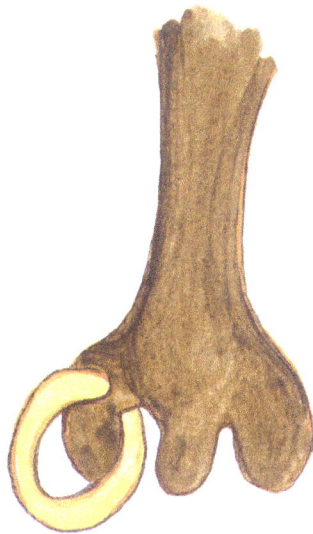

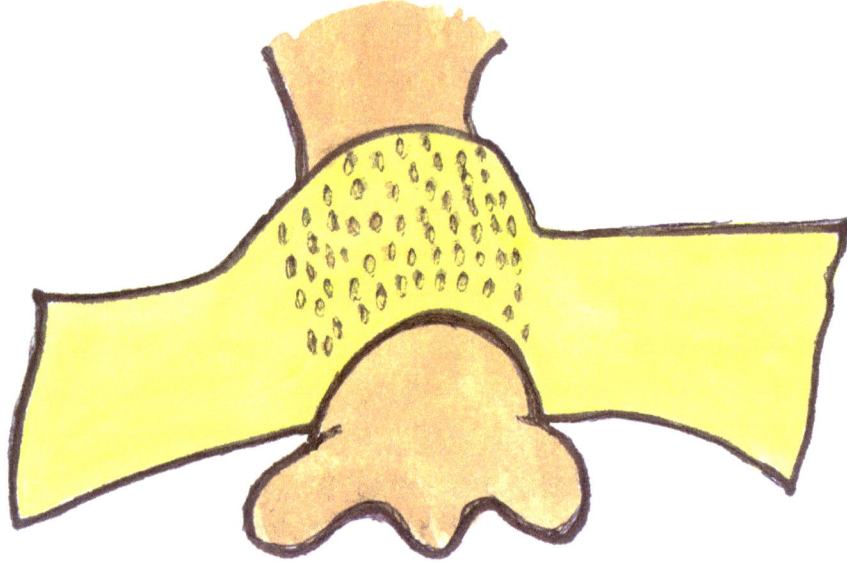

Some
noses
endure
rhinoplasty.

Some
noses
are
clogged

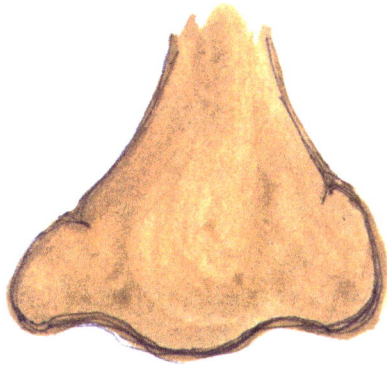

and
some
waterlogged

and
some
just
smell smells
that are
nasty.

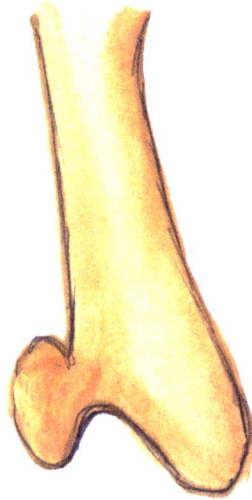

Some
noses
sense
delightful aromas,

some
stuck up ones
point
toward
the sky.

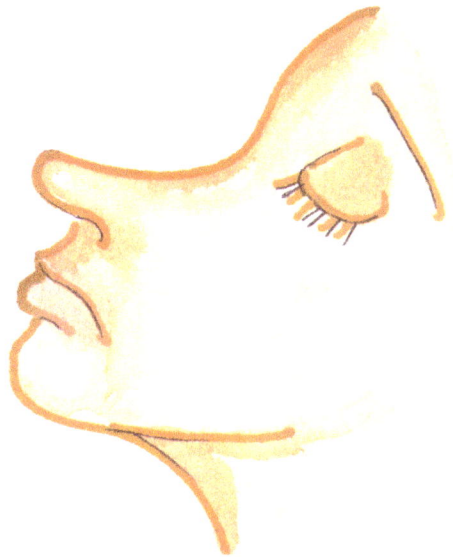

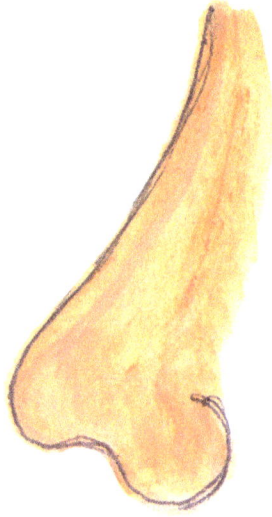

Some
noses
are pert

and

some

noses

hurt

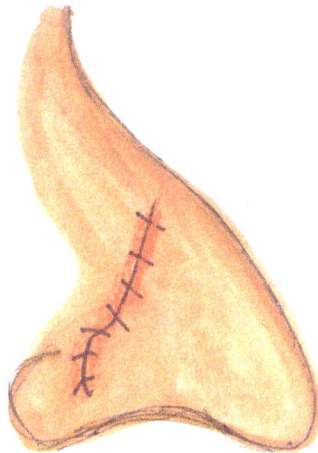

and
others
just drip
when
you cry.

Now, I think you can see from the previous words

that
a rose
is a flower
that
grows.

And

so,

while

a

rose

is always

a

rose

a

nose

s'not

a

nose

s'not

a

nose.

www.ingramcontent.com/pod-product-compliance
Lightning Source LLC
Chambersburg PA
CBHW060901090426
42738CB00025B/3489